Early Praise for *Pandas Brain Teasers*

Miki is a world-class Python and Go expert and a hands-on professional. This publication is more evidence that he comes from the field and that he can articulate not only the practical benefits and their practice but also the thought and the meta thinking behind them.

➤ **Shlomo Yona**
  Founder and Chief Scientist, mathematic.ai

Even after several years of working with pandas, and thinking I've hit every rock in the road, *Pandas Brain Teasers* managed to surprise me and teach me about pandas.

➤ **Uri Goren**
  Recommendation System Expert/Natural Language Processing, argmax

This book is a fun and intellectually stimulating resource for programmers who wish to gain an in-depth understanding of Python's Pandas package. It is highly recommended, especially for data scientists and data analysts, but will undoubtedly prove beneficial for any programmer who works with data.

➤ **Iddo Berger**
  CTO, Superfly Insights

A real jam!

➤ **Luis Voloch**
  CTO, Cofounder, Immunai

Pandas Brain Teasers

Exercise Your Mind

Miki Tebeka

The Pragmatic Bookshelf

Raleigh, North Carolina

Many of the designations used by manufacturers and sellers to distinguish their products are claimed as trademarks. Where those designations appear in this book, and The Pragmatic Programmers, LLC was aware of a trademark claim, the designations have been printed in initial capital letters or in all capitals. The Pragmatic Starter Kit, The Pragmatic Programmer, Pragmatic Programming, Pragmatic Bookshelf, PragProg and the linking *g* device are trademarks of The Pragmatic Programmers, LLC.

Every precaution was taken in the preparation of this book. However, the publisher assumes no responsibility for errors or omissions, or for damages that may result from the use of information (including program listings) contained herein.

For our complete catalog of hands-on, practical, and Pragmatic content for software developers, please visit *https://pragprog.com*.

The team that produced this book includes:

CEO: Dave Rankin
COO: Janet Furlow
Managing Editor: Tammy Coron
Development Editor: Margaret Eldridge
Copy Editor: Jennifer Whipple
Indexing: Potomac Indexing, LLC
Layout: Gilson Graphics
Founders: Andy Hunt and Dave Thomas

For sales, volume licensing, and support, please contact *support@pragprog.com*.

For international rights, please contact *rights@pragprog.com*.

ISBN-13: 978-1-68050-901-4
Book version: P1.0—September 2021

To all the data nerds out there, you rock!

Contents

Part I — Pandas Brain Teasers

Acknowledgments

I'm grateful for anyone who helped me write this book. Every contribution, from finding bugs to fixing grammar to letting me work in peace, was super helpful.

Here is a list of people who helped. My apologies to anyone I forgot:

- Iddo Berger
- Luis Voloch
- Shlomo Yona
- Uri Goren

Preface

Pandas is a great library. I have used it in many projects, and it always delivers. Like any big project, the Pandas developers had to make some design decisions that at times seem surprising. This book uses these quirks as a teaching opportunity. By understanding the gaps in your knowledge, you'll become better at what you do.

There's a lot of research showing that people who make mistakes during the learning process learn better than people who don't. If you use this approach when fixing bugs, you'll find you enjoy bug hunting more and become a better developer after each bug you fix.

These teasers will help you avoid mistakes. Some of the teasers are from my own experience shipping bugs to production and some are from others doing the same.

Teasers are fun! We geeks love to solve puzzles. You can also use these teasers to impress your coworkers, have knowledge competitions, and become better together.

Many of these brain teasers are from quizzes I gave at conferences and meetups. I've found that people highly enjoy them, and they tend to liven up the room.

At the beginning of each chapter, I'll show you a short Python program with Pandas code in it and ask you to guess the output. These are the possible answers:

- Syntax error
- Exception
- Some output (e.g., [1 2 3])

Versions

 I'm using Python version 3.8.3 and Pandas version 1.0.5. The output *might* change in future versions.

Before moving on to the answer and the explanation, go ahead and guess the output. After guessing, I encourage you to run the code and see the output yourself; only then proceed to read the solution and the explanation. I've been teaching programming for many years and found this course of action to be highly effective.

About the Author

Miki Tebeka has a B.Sc. in computer science from Ben Gurion University. He also studied there toward an M.Sc. in computational linguistics.

Miki has a passion for teaching and mentoring. He teaches many workshops on various technical subjects all over the world and has mentored many young developers on their way to success. Miki is involved in open source, has several projects of his own, and has contributed to several more, including the Python project. He has been using Python for more than twenty-three years now.

Miki wrote *Python Brain Teasers*, *Go Brain Teasers*, and *Forging Python* and is a LinkedIn Learning author and an organizer of Go Israel Meetup, GopherCon Israel, and PyData Israel Conference.

About the Code

You can find the brain teasers code at https://pragprog.com/titles/d-pandas/pandas-brain-teasers/.

I've tried to keep the code as short as possible and remove anything that is not related to the teaser. This is *not* how you'll normally write code.

Some code examples are shown in the IPython interactive prompt. You should write the following two imports in your IPython session to follow the examples:

```
In [1]: import pandas as pd
In [2]: import numpy as np
```

When referring to a brain teaser, I assume you ran the code with the %run magic. For example

```
In [3]: %run sanchez.py
```

This will load all the variables defined in the file into your IPython, even if there was an exception.

About You

I assume you know Pandas at some level and have experience programming with it. This book is not for learning how to work with Pandas. If you don't know Pandas, I recommend learning it first (it's fun). There are many resources online. I recommend the official documentation and the book *Python for Data Analysis* by Pandas initial developer Wes McKinney.

One More Thing

As you work through the puzzles in this book, it might help to picture yourself as Nancy Drew, Sherlock Holmes, or any other of your favorite detectives trying to solve a murder mystery in which *you* are the murderer. Think of it like this:

> Debugging is like being a detective in a crime movie where you're also the murderer.
>
> — Filipe Fortes

With this mindset, I have found that things are easier to understand, and the work is more enjoyable. So, with that in mind, have fun guessing the brain teasers in this book—perhaps you might even learn a new trick or two.

If you'd like to learn more, please send an email to info@353solutions.com, and we'll tailor a hands-on workshop to meet your needs. There's also a comprehensive offering of hands-on workshops at https://www.353solutions.com.

Stay curious, and keep hacking!

Miki Tebeka, March 2020

Part I

Pandas Brain Teasers

Rectified

relu.py
```python
import pandas as pd

def relu(n):
    if n < 0:
        return 0
    return n

arr = pd.Series([-1, 0, 1])
print(relu(arr))
```

Guess the Output

 Try to guess what the output is before moving to the next page.

This code will raise a ValueError.

The problematic line is if n < 0:. n is the result of arr < 0, which is a pandas.Series.

```
In [1]: import pandas as pd
In [2]: arr = pd.Series([-1, 0, 1])
In [3]: arr < 0
Out[3]:
0     True
1     False
2     False
dtype: bool
```

Once arr < 0 is computed, you use it in an if statement, which brings us to how Boolean values work in Python.

Every Python object, not just True and False, has a Boolean value. The documentation states the rules:

Everything is True except

- 0 numbers: 0, 0.0, 0+0j, ...
- Empty collections: [], {}, '', ...
- None
- False

You can test the truth value of a Python object using the built-in bool function.

In addition to these rules, any object can state its own Boolean value using the _bool_ special method. The Boolean logic for a pandas.Series is different from the one for a list or a tuple; it raises an exception.

```
In [4]: bool(arr < 0)
...
ValueError: The truth value of a Series is ambiguous.
Use a.empty, a.bool(), a.item(), a.any() or a.all().
```

The exception tells you the reasoning. It follows "The Zen of Python," which states the following:

> In the face of ambiguity, refuse the temptation to guess.

So what are your options? You can use all or any but then you'll need to check the type of n to see if it's a plain number of a pandas.Series.

A function that works both on scalar and a pandas.Series (or a numpy array) is called a ufunc, short for *universal function*. Most of the functions from numpy or Pandas, such as min or to_datetime, are ufuncs.

numpy has a vectorize decorator for these cases.

```
relu_vec.py
import numpy as np
import pandas as pd

@np.vectorize
def relu(n):
    if n < 0:
        return 0
    return n

arr = pd.Series([-1, 0, 1])
print(relu(arr))
```

Now, relu will work both on scalars (e.g., 7, 2.18, ...) and vectors (e.g., numpy array, pandas.Series, ...)

Watch Your Types

 The output of relu now is numpy.ndarray, not pandas.Series as well.

Further Reading

Truth Value Testing in the Python Documentation
> docs.python.org/3/library/stdtypes.html#truth-value-testing

PEP 285
> python.org/dev/peps/pep-0285/

bool Type Documentation
> docs.python.org/3/reference/datamodel.html#object.__bool__

Universal Functions on the numpy Docs
> numpy.org/doc/stable/reference/ufuncs.html?highlight=ufunc

"The Zen of Python"
> python.org/dev/peps/pep-0020/#the-zen-of-python

numpy.vectorize
> numpy.org/doc/stable/reference/generated/numpy.vectorize.html#numpy.vectorize

numba.vectorize
> numba.pydata.org/numba-doc/latest/user/vectorize.html

In or Out?

simpsons.py

```
import pandas as pd

simpsons = pd.Series(
    ['Homer', 'Marge', 'Bart', 'Lisa', 'Maggie'])
print('Bart' in simpsons)
```

Guess the Output

 Try to guess what the output is before moving to the next page.

This code will print: False

pandas.Series is a sequence type. Most Python sequences are indexed by a range, meaning the first item is at index 0, the second item is at index 1, and so forth.

0 vs. 1

Python is a 0-based language. Some languages, such as MATLAB, are 1-based. The compromise to use ½ as the first index didn't go well. :)

pandas.Series (and pandas.DataFrame) indices are more flexible. The default is a range-based index, but there are other types of indices.

```
In [1]: import pandas as pd
In [2]: pd.Series([1,2,3,4], index=['a', 'b', 'b', 'c'])
Out[2]:
a    1
b    2
b    3
c    4
dtype: int64
```

The previous example index has strings as labels. Note that the labels don't have to be unique.

```
In [3]: pd.Series([1,2,3,4], index=pd.date_range('2020', periods=4))
Out[3]:
2020-01-01    1
2020-01-02    2
2020-01-03    3
2020-01-04    4
Freq: D, dtype: int64
```

This series has a pandas.DatetimeIndex index. Indexing with pandas.DatetimeIndex enables a lot of time series operations, such as up-sampling, down-sampling, and more.

These kinds of indices make a pandas.Series behave as a dict as well.

```
In [4]: s = pd.Series([1,2,3], index=['a', 'b', 'c'])
In [5]: s['c']
Out[5]: 3
```

This allows two choices for the in operator: either behave like a sequence (e.g., list, tuple) or like a dict. The design choice was to have in behave like a dict and check in the keys that are the index labels.

"in" Performance

 The in operator of pandas.Series is very slow compared to the built-in dict. On my machine it's about fifteen times slower.

How *can* you check if a pandas.Series contains a value? Here is one option:

```
In [6]: 'Bart' in simpsons.values
Out[6]: True
```

.values returns the underlying numpy array, where the in operator works as expected.

Further Reading

Sequence Types on the Python Documentation
    docs.python.org/3/library/stdtypes.html#sequence-types-list-tuple-range

Indexing and Selecting Data in the Pandas Documentation
    pandas.pydata.org/pandas-docs/stable/user_guide/indexing.html

__contains__ Special Method
    docs.python.org/3/reference/datamodel.html#object.__contains__

Month by Month

```
monthly.py
from io import StringIO
import pandas as pd

csv_data = '''\
day,hits
2020-01-01,400
2020-02-02,800
2020-02-03,600
'''

df = pd.read_csv(StringIO(csv_data))
print(df['day'].dt.month.unique())
```

Guess the Output

Try to guess what the output is before moving to the next page.

This code will raise an AttributeError.

The comma-separated values (CSV) format does not have a schema. Everything you read from it is a string. Pandas does a great job of "guessing" the types of data inside the CSV, but sometimes it needs help.

You can use .dtypes to see what types a DataFrame has:

```
In [3]: df.dtypes
Out[3]:
day      object
hits      int64
dtype: object
```

The object dtype usually means a str (Python's string). The read_csv function has many parameters, including parse_dates.

monthly_parse.py
```
from io import StringIO
import pandas as pd

csv_data = '''\
day,hits
2020-01-01,400
2020-02-02,800
2020-02-03,600
'''

df = pd.read_csv(StringIO(csv_data), parse_dates=['day'])
print(df['day'].dt.month.unique())
```

parse_dates uses the dateutil parser, which can handle many formats. But it needs help sometimes: is 1/5/2020 January 5 (US format) or May 1 (EU format)? You can use the day_first parameter to read_csv, or better, pick a time format that is unambiguous like RFC 3339 (e.g., 2020-01-05T10:20:30).

I prefer not to use CSV and reach out to other formats (such as SQL, HDF5, ...) whenever possible.

Further Reading

read_csv Documentation
    pandas.pydata.org/pandas-docs/stable/reference/api/pandas.read_csv.html

IO Tools in Pandas Documentation
    pandas.pydata.org/pandas-docs/stable/user_guide/io.html

Comma-Separated Values on Wikipedia
en.wikipedia.org/wiki/Comma-separated_values

dateutil.parser Documentation
dateutil.readthedocs.io/en/stable/parser.html

RFC 3339
https://www.ietf.org/rfc/rfc3339.txt

Round and Round We Go

round.py
```python
import pandas as pd

s = pd.Series([-2.5, -1.5, -0.5, 0.5, 1.5, 2.5])
print(s.round())
```

Guess the Output

Try to guess what the output is before moving to the next page.

This code will print the following:

```
0   -2.0
1   -2.0
2   -0.0
3    0.0
4    2.0
5    2.0
dtype: float64
```

Rounding seems easy. round(1.1) evaluates to 1 and round(1.8) evaluates to 2. The question is, how do you round the .5 numbers? Should you round up? Down? Turns out, there are a lot of ways to do it.

Python 3 uses *bankers' rounding*. Odd numbers are rounded up, even numbers are rounded down. The reasoning behind this method is that if you round a list of numbers, assuming there's roughly the same number of odd and even numbers, the error (rounding) will cancel each other.

Further Reading

Rounding on Wikipedia
> en.wikipedia.org/wiki/Rounding

round Documentation
> https://docs.python.org/3/library/functions.html#round

Floating-Point Arithmetic: Issues and Limitations in the Python Tutorial
> docs.python.org/3/tutorial/floatingpoint.html#tut-fp-issues

Let's Get Schwifty

sanchez.py

```python
import pandas as pd

s = pd.Series(['Rick', 'Morty', 'Summer', 'Beth', 'Jerry'])
print(s.lower())
```

Guess the Output

 Try to guess what the output is before moving to the next page.

This code will raise an AttributeError.

The pandas.Series has a lot of methods:

```
In [1]: import pandas as pd
In [2]: sum(1 for attr in dir(pd.Series) if attr[0] != '_')
Out[2]: 207
```

But lower is not one of them:

```
In [3]: hasattr(pd.Series, 'lower')
Out[3]: False
```

Most of the time, people use Pandas with numerical data. The Pandas developers decided to move non-numerical methods out of the (already big) pandas.Series top-level API. To make the teaser code work, use the .str attribute:

sanchez_str.py
```
import pandas as pd

s = pd.Series(['Rick', 'Morty', 'Summer', 'Beth', 'Jerry'])
print(s.str.lower())
```

pandas.Series (and pandas.DataFrame) has several such special attribute accessors:

- .str for string methods such as lower, match, ...
- .dt to work with datetime/timestamp data (e.g., s.dt.year)
- .cat to work with categorical data
- .sparse to work with sparse data

Further Reading

pandas.Series Documentation
    pandas.pydata.org/pandas-docs/stable/reference/series.html

str.lower Documentation
    pandas.pydata.org/pandas-docs/stable/reference/api/pandas.Series.str.lower.html

Working with Text Data in the Pandas Documentation
    pandas.pydata.org/docs/user_guide/text.html

Time Series / Date Functionality in the Pandas Documentation
    pandas.pydata.org/pandas-docs/stable/user_guide/timeseries.html

Categorical Data in the Pandas Documentation
    pandas.pydata.org/pandas-docs/stable/user_guide/categorical.html

Sparse Data in the Pandas Documentation
    pandas.pydata.org/docs/user_guide/sparse.html

Full of It

empty.py

```python
import pandas as pd

s = pd.Series([], dtype='float64')
print('full' if s.all() else 'empty')
```

Guess the Output

Try to guess what the output is before moving to the next page.

This code will print: full

The pandas.Series.all documentation says the following:

> Return whether all elements are True, potentially over an axis.

> Returns True unless there is at least one element within a series or along a DataFrame axis that is False or equivalent (e.g., zero or empty).

The second paragraph explains what we see. There are no False elements in the empty series. The built-in all function behaves the same:

```
In [1]: all([])
Out[1]: True
```

all is like the mathematical ∀ (for all) symbol. Here's what Wikipedia says:

> By convention, the formula $\forall x \in \varnothing, P(x)$ is always true, regardless of the formula $P(x)$ ...

The any function has the same logic, only reversed. It implies "there exists at least one element," which in the case of the empty sequence is always False:

```
In [1]: import pandas as pd
In [2]: import numpy as np
In [3]: any([])
Out[3]: False
In [5]: pd.Series([], dtype=np.float64).any()
Out[5]: False
```

Further Reading

pandas.Series.all Documentation
    pandas.pydata.org/pandas-docs/stable/reference/api/pandas.Series.all.html

pandas.Series.any Documentation
    pandas.pydata.org/pandas-docs/stable/reference/api/pandas.Series.any.html

Empty Set on Wikipedia
    en.wikipedia.org/wiki/Universal_quantification#The_empty_set

Universal Quantification on Wikipedia
    en.wikipedia.org/wiki/Universal_quantification

Existential Quantification on Wikipedia
    en.wikipedia.org/wiki/Existential_quantification

A Delicious Div Sum

```python
import pandas as pd

v1 = pd.Series([0, 2, 4])
v2 = pd.Series([0, 1, 2])
out = v1 // v2
print(out.sum())
```

Guess the Output

 Try to guess what the output is before moving to the next page.

This code will print: 4.0

There are a few things going on in this teaser. The first is the // operator in out = v1 // v2. This is the floordiv operator in Python. Unlike the regular division, it returns an int.

```
In [1]: 7/2
Out[1]: 3.5
In [2]: 7//2
Out[2]: 3
```

The // operator is useful when you want to calculate indices (e.g., in a binary search).

The next odd thing is that we managed to divide by 0. If you try to divide by 0 in the Python shell, it'll fail:

```
In [3]: 1/0
...
ZeroDivisionError: division by zero
```

Pandas, and the underlying numpy array, is using different numbers than Python. The reason is that Python numbers are Python objects and take a lot of space compared to machine numbers. Python numbers can grow as much as you want, while Pandas/numpy numbers are limited to their size in bits.

```
In [4]: 2<<100
Out[4]: 2535301200456458802993406410752
In [4]: np.int64(2)<<100
Out[4]: 0
```

<< is the left shift operator.

You can see that the type of v1 and v2 is int64:

```
In [5]: v1.dtype
Out[5]: dtype('int64')
```

This gives you a clue why the division by 0 worked:

```
In [6]: np.int64(0)/np.int64(0)
<ipython-input-62-76db10acbf60>:1: RuntimeWarning: invalid value encountered
  in long_scalars np.int64(0)/np.int64(0)
Out[6]: nan
```

There is a warning but we get a nan. nan is a special float value meaning *not a number*. It's usually used to indicate missing values. Since integers don't have a special *empty* value, Pandas changed the dtype of out to float64.

```
In [7]: out.dtype
Out[7]: dtype('float64')
```

Bugs Ahoy

 This dtype change can lead to some interesting bugs. Watch out for it!

In newer versions of Pandas, there's a new IntegerArray type that can have missing values. Pandas has several more *missing* types. For example, there's NaT for missing time. You can use the pandas.isnull function to check for missing values.

The last item on the agenda is summing up a series with nan values. If you're coming from numpy, you'd expect a nan as a result.

```
In [8]: out.values
Out[8]: array([nan,  2.,  2.])
In [9]: out.values.sum()
Out[9]: nan
```

In numpy, you need to use nansum to ignore nan values.

```
In [10]: np.nansum(out.values)
Out[10]: 4.0
```

Pandas takes a different approach. It sees nan more as a missing value than *not a number* and tends to ignore it in most operations.

```
In [11]: out.sum()
Out[11]: 4.0
```

Further Reading

floordiv Operator
    docs.python.org/3/library/operator.html#operator.floordiv

PEP 238: Division Operator
    python.org/dev/peps/pep-0238/

Data Types in the numpy Documentation
    numpy.org/devdocs/user/basics.types.html

IntegerArray in the Pandas Documentation
    pandas.pydata.org/pandas-docs/stable/reference/api/pandas.arrays.IntegerArray.html

Working with Missing Data in the Pandas Documentation
    pandas.pydata.org/pandas-docs/stable/user_guide/missing_data.html

Bitwise Operators on the Python Wiki
    wiki.python.org/moin/BitwiseOperators

Once Upon a Time

times.py

```python
import pandas as pd

s1 = pd.to_datetime([
    '2020-01-01T00:00:00+00:00',
    '2020-02-02T00:00:00+00:00',
    '2020-03-03T00:00:00+00:00',
])
s2 = pd.Series([
    pd.Timestamp(2020, 1, 1),
    pd.Timestamp(2020, 2, 2),
    pd.Timestamp(2020, 3, 3),
])
print(s1 == s2)
```

Guess the Output

Try to guess what the output is before moving to the next page.

This code will raise a TypeError.

In Pandas (and Python) there is one Timestamp (or datetime) type. However, it is divided into two subtypes: naive and tz-aware. The naive type doesn't have time-zone information associated with it, while the tz-aware type does.

You cannot compare naive and tz-aware values:

```
In [1]: t = pd.Timestamp(2020, 5, 23)
In [2]: t
Out[2]: Timestamp('2020-05-23 00:00:00')
In [3]: ut = t.tz_localize('UTC')
In [4]: ut
Out[4]: Timestamp('2020-05-23 00:00:00+0000', tz='UTC')
In [5]: ut == t
...
TypeError: Cannot compare tz-naive and tz-aware timestamps
```

This is the cause of exception in this teaser.

You *must* work with tz-aware timestamps if you want to convert from one time zone to another.

```
In [6]: t.tz_convert('US/Pacific')
...
TypeError: Cannot convert tz-naive Timestamp, use tz_localize to localize
In [7]: ut.tz_convert('US/Pacific')
Out[7]: Timestamp('2020-05-22 17:00:00-0700', tz='US/Pacific')
```

Time-Zone Database

 As of Python 3.8, Python itself does not come with a time-zone database. Pandas depends on the "pytz" package that comes with a time-zone database and updates periodically. Since Python 3.9, there is a new built-in "zoneinfo" module.

Further Reading

Time-Zone Handling in the Pandas Documentation
> pandas.pydata.org/pandas-docs/stable/user_guide/timeseries.html#time-zone-handling

pandas.Timestamp Documentation
> pandas.pydata.org/pandas-docs/stable/reference/api/pandas.Timestamp.html

pytz Package
> pythonhosted.org/pytz/

PEP 615: IANA Time-Zone Database in the Standard Library
python.org/dev/peps/pep-0615/

Time Zone on Wikipedia
en.wikipedia.org/wiki/Time_zone

Falsehoods Programmers Believe About Time
infiniteundo.com/post/25326999628/falsehoods-programmers-believe-about-time

A Hefty Bonus

grades.py

```
import pandas as pd

grades = pd.Series([61, 82, 57])
bonuses = pd.Series([10, 5, 10, 10])
out = grades + bonuses
print(out)
```

Guess the Output

 Try to guess what the output is before moving to the next page.

This code will print:

```
0    71.0
1    87.0
2    67.0
3     NaN
dtype: float64</code></pre></td>
```

`pandas.Series` and `numpy.ndarray` are different from Python lists. The + operator on Python lists does concatenation:

```
In [1]: [1, 2, 3] + [4, 5]
Out[1]: [1, 2, 3, 4, 5]
```

`numpy.ndarray`, and `pandas.Series` that is built on it, has a different behavior. They will do element-wise operations and will try to match the dimensions as much as possible (known as *broadcasting*).

```
In [2]: np.array([1,2,3]) + np.array([4,5,6])
Out[2]: array([5, 7, 9])
In [3]: np.array([1,2,3]) + 3
Out[3]: array([4, 5, 6])
```

If numpy can't broadcast, it'll raise an error.

```
In [4]: np.array([1,2,3]) + np.array([4,5,6,7])
...
ValueError: operands could not be broadcast together with shapes (3,) (4,)
```

This is where Pandas diverges from numpy. The `pandas.Series` (and `pandas.DataFrame`) uses labels for matching elements (somewhat like SQL join).

```
In [5]: s1 = pd.Series([1,2,3], index=['a', 'b', 'c'])
In [6]: s2 = pd.Series([10,20,30], index=['c', 'b', 'a'])
In [7]: s1 + s2
Out[7]:
a    31
b    22
c    13
dtype: int64
```

When Pandas can't find a matching label, it'll use `nan` for a value. This is what happens in this teaser.

Further Reading

Matching/Broadcasting Behavior in the Pandas Documentation
    pandas.pydata.org/pandas-docs/stable/getting_started/basics.html#matching-broadcasting-behavior

Broadcasting in the numpy Documentation
numpy.org/doc/stable/user/basics.broadcasting.html

"Losing Your Loops" (video demonstration on what you can do with broadcasting)
youtube.com/watch?v=EEUXKG97YRw

SQL Join on Wikipedia
en.wikipedia.org/wiki/Join_(SQL

Emulating Container Types in the Python Documentation
docs.python.org/3/reference/datamodel.html#emulating-container-types

Free Range

in_range.py
```
import pandas as pd

nums = pd.Series([1, 2, 3, 4, 5, 6])
print(nums[(nums > 2) and (nums < 5)])
```

Guess the Output

Try to guess what the output is before moving to the next page.

This code will raise a ValueError.

The result of nums>2 is a series of Boolean values:

```
In [1]: nums>2
Out[1]:
0    False
1    False
2     True
3     True
4     True
5     True
dtype: bool
```

We can use this Boolean series to select parts of a series with the same size, including, of course, nums.

```
In [2]: nums[nums>2]
Out[2]:
2    3
3    4
4    5
5    6
dtype: int64
```

This is known as Boolean indexing.

In some cases, you'd want to combine two or more of these Boolean series to create a more complex condition. Coming from Python, you're familiar with the and, or, and not logical operators. This is what we're doing in the teaser (nums > 2) and (nums < 5). However, these Python logical operators will call the built-in bool function on nums > 2 and nums<5.

As you saw in the puzzle *Rectified*, this will raise an error. To solve this, Pandas and numpy use the bitwise operators:

- & instead of and
- | instead of or
- ~ instead of not

For example, the following will pick all the non-nan values in a series:

```
In [3]: s = pd.Series([1, np.nan, 2])
In [4]: s[~pd.isnull(s)]
Out[4444]:
0    1.0
2    2.0
dtype: float64
```

To fix our teaser, replace the and with &:

in_range_bitwise.py
```
import pandas as pd

nums = pd.Series([1, 2, 3, 4, 5, 6])
print(nums[(nums > 2) & (nums < 5)])
```

Further Reading

Bitwise Operators on the Python Wiki
> wiki.python.org/moin/BitwiseOperators

Boolean Indexing in the Pandas Documentation
> pandas.pydata.org/pandas-docs/stable/user_guide/indexing.html#boolean-indexing

Boolean Array Indexing in the numpy Documentation
> numpy.org/devdocs/reference/arrays.indexing.html

Phil? Nah!?

fillna.py

```
import numpy as np
import pandas as pd

s = pd.Series([1, 2, np.nan, 4, 5])
s.fillna(3)
print(s.sum())
```

Guess the Output

Try to guess what the output is before moving to the next page.

This code will print: 12.0

The pandas.Series.fillna documentation says the following:

> *Returns*: Series or None
>   Object with missing values filled or None if inplace=True.

It's always a good idea to not change (mutate) an object passed to a function. On the other hand, Pandas tries to be efficient and not copy data around a lot.

The design decision for fillna, both in pandas.Series and pandas.DataFrame, was not to change the original object and return a copy. But the user has an option to pass inplace=True, and then the original object is changed.

When a method changes an object, the common practice in Python is to return None. Other languages, such as JavaScript, prefer to return the object, allowing method chaining.

If you change line 5 to s.fillna(3, inplace=True), you'll see 15.0 as the output.

fillna will work on anything that is considered a missing value: numpy.nan, pandas.NA, pandas.NaT, None …

Empty strings or collections are not considered missing values.

Further Reading

pandas.Series.fillna Documentation
    pandas.pydata.org/pandas-docs/stable/reference/api/pandas.Series.fillna.html

Working with Missing Data in the Pandas Documentation
    pandas.pydata.org/pandas-docs/stable/user_guide/missing_data.html

Method Chaining on Wikipedia
    en.wikipedia.org/wiki/Method_chaining

Multiplying

mul.py
```python
import pandas as pd

v = pd.Series([.1, 1., 1.1])
out = v * v
expected = pd.Series([.01, 1., 1.21])
if (out == expected).all():
    print('Math rocks!')
else:
    print('Please reinstall universe & reboot.')
```

Guess the Output

Try to guess what the output is before moving to the next page.

This code will print: Please reinstall universe & reboot.

out == expected returns a Boolean pandas.Series. The all method returns True if all elements are True.

When you look at out and expected, they *seem* the same:

```
In [1]: out
Out[1]:
0    0.01
1    1.00
2    1.21
dtype: float64
In [2]: expected
Out[2]:
0    0.01
1    1.00
2    1.21
dtype: float64
```

But when we compare, we see something strange:

```
In [2]: out == expected
Out[2]:
0    False
1     True
2    False
dtype: bool
```

Only the middle value (1.0) is equal.

Looking deeper, we see the problem:

```
In [3]: print(out[2])
1.2100000000000002
```

There is a difference between how Pandas is showing the value and how print does.

String Representation

 Always remember that the string representation of an object is not the object itself. This is beautifully illustrated by the painting *The Treachery of Images.*

Some new developers, when seeing this or similar issues, come to the message boards and say, "We found a bug in Pandas!" The usual answer is, "Read the fine manual" (RTFM).

> Floating point is sort of like quantum physics: the closer you look, the messier it gets.

— Grant Edwards

The basic idea behind this issue is that floating points sacrifice accuracy for speed (i.e., cheat). Don't be shocked. It's a trade-off we do a lot in computer science.

The result you see conforms with the floating-point specification. If you run the same code in Go, Rust, C, Java, ... you will see the same output.

If you want to learn more about floating points, see the links in the following section. The main point you need to remember is that they are not accurate, and accuracy worsens as the number gets bigger.

You're going to work a lot with floating points and will need to compare pandas.Series or pandas.DataFrame. Don't expect everything to be exactly equal; think of an acceptable threshold and use the numpy.allclose function.

```
In [4]: import numpy as np
In [5]: np.allclose(out, expected)
Out[5]: True
```

numpy.allclose has many options you can tweak. See the documentation.

```python
mul_ac.py
import numpy as np
import pandas as pd

v = pd.Series([.1, 1., 1.1])
out = v * v
expected = pd.Series([.01, 1., 1.21])
if np.allclose(out, expected):
    print('Math rocks!')
else:
    print('Please reinstall universe & reboot.')
```

If you need better accuracy, look into the decimal module, which provides correctly rounded decimal floating-point arithmetic.

Further Reading

Floating-Point Arithmetic: Issues and Limitations in the Python Documentation
  docs.python.org/3/tutorial/floatingpoint.html

floating point zine by Julia Evans
  twitter.com/b0rk/status/986424989648936960

What Every Computer Scientist Should Know About Floating-Point Arithmetic
docs.oracle.com/cd/E19957-01/806-3568/ncg_goldberg.html

numpy.allclose Documentation
docs.scipy.org/doc/numpy/reference/generated/numpy.allclose.html

Built-in decimal Module
docs.python.org/3/library/decimal.html

A 10% Discount

discount.py

```python
import pandas as pd

df = pd.DataFrame([
    ['Bugs', True, 72.3],
    ['Daffy', False, 30.7],
    ['Tweety', True, 23.5],
    ['Elmer', False, 103.9],
], columns=['Customer', 'Member', 'Amount'])

df[df['Member']]['Amount'] *= 0.9
print(df)
```

Guess the Output

Try to guess what the output is before moving to the next page.

This code will print a warning and then

```
Customer  Member  Amount
0     Bugs    True     72.3
1    Daffy   False     30.7
2   Tweety    True     23.5
3    Elmer   False    103.9</code></pre></td>
```

The change is not reflected in df. The reason is that Pandas does a lot of work under the hood to avoid copying data. However, in some cases it can't, and then you'll get a copy of the data.

The warning is very helpful; sadly, a lot of developers ignore it.

```
discount.py:11: SettingWithCopyWarning:
A value is trying to be set on a copy of a slice from a DataFrame.
Try using .loc[row_indexer,col_indexer] = value instead

See the caveats in the documentation: https://pandas.pydata.org/pandas-docs...
```

You have both the solution and a link to more information—got to love the Pandas developers. It's also a good indication that many developers face this issue.

Let's apply the warning suggestion to our code:

discount_loc.py
```python
import pandas as pd

df = pd.DataFrame([
    ['Bugs', True, 72.3],
    ['Daffy', False, 30.7],
    ['Tweety', True, 23.5],
    ['Elmer', False, 103.9],
], columns=['Customer', 'Member', 'Amount'])

df.loc[df['Member'], 'Amount'] *= 0.9
print(df)
```

This will print the expected output without a warning:

```
        Customer  Membership  Amount
0     Bugs          True    65.07
1    Daffy         False    30.70
2   Tweety          True    21.15
3    Elmer         False   103.90
```

Further Reading

Returning a View Versus a Copy in the Pandas Documentation
pandas.pydata.org/pandas-docs/stable/user_guide/indexing.html#returning-a-view-versus-a-copy

DataFrame.loc Documentation
pandas.pydata.org/pandas-docs/stable/reference/api/pandas.DataFrame.loc.html

A Tale of One City

population.py
```
import pandas as pd

cities = pd.DataFrame([
    ('Vienna', 'Austria', 1_899_055),
    ('Sofia', 'Bulgaria', 1_238_438),
    ('Tekirdağ', 'Turkey', 1_055_412),
], columns=['City', 'Country', 'Population'])

def population_of(city):
    return cities[cities['City'] == city]['Population']

city = 'Tekirdag˘'
print(population_of(city))
```

Guess the Output

Try to guess what the output is before moving to the next page.

This code will print: Series([], Name: Population, dtype: int64)

The output means we can't find Tekirdağ in the cities DataFrame. But ... it's right there!

Let's investigate:

```
In [1]: city
Out[1]: 'Tekirdag˘'
In [2]: city2 = cities.loc[2]['City']
In [3]: city2
Out[3]: 'Tekirdağ'
In [4]: city2 == city
Out[4]: False
```

Hmm ...

```
In [5]: len(city)
Out[5]: 9
In [6]: len(city2)
Out[6]: 8
```

Hello Unicode, my old friend ...

Unicode

 The Unicode issue might not render well in the book. Look at the source code to see exactly what's going on.

In the beginning, computers were developed in English-speaking countries: the UK and the US. When early developers wanted to encode text in ways that computers can understand, they came out with the following scheme. Use a byte (8 bits) to represent a character. For example, a is 97 (01100001), b is 98, and so on. One byte is enough for the English alphabet, containing twenty-six lowercase letters, twenty-six uppercase letters, and ten digits. There is even some space left for other special characters (e.g., 9 for tab). This is known as ASCII encoding.

After a while, other countries started to use computers and wanted support for their native languages. ASCII wasn't good enough. A single byte can't hold all the numbers needed to represent letters in different languages. This led to several different encoding schemes. The most common one is UTF-8.

Some of the characters in UTF-8 are control characters. In city we have the character g at position 7, and after it a control character saying "add a breve to the previous character." This is why the length of city is 9. city2 from the cities DataFrame has ğ at location 7.

These are known as Unicode normalization forms. You can use the unicodedata module to normalize strings to the same format.

On top of that, people might want to do case-insensitive searches for cities. In some cases, with Unicode, str.lower or str.upper methods won't do the job you think. You should use the str.casefold method.

Here's a solution to this teaser incorporating all of these methods:

population_norm.py
```
import unicodedata

import pandas as pd

cities = pd.DataFrame([
    ('Vienna', 'Austria', 1_899_055),
    ('Sofia', 'Bulgaria', 1_238_438),
    ('Tekirdağ', 'Turkey', 1_055_412),
], columns=['City', 'Country', 'Population'])


def population_of(city):
    city = normalize(city)
    return cities[cities['city_norm'] == city]['Population']


def normalize(name):
    return unicodedata.normalize('NFKC', name).casefold()


cities['city_norm'] = cities['City'].apply(normalize)

city = 'Tekirdag˘'
print(population_of(city))
```

Further Reading

ASCII on Wikipedia
　　en.wikipedia.org/wiki/ASCII

UTF-8 on Wikipedia
　　en.wikipedia.org/wiki/UTF-8

Unicode HOWTO
　　docs.python.org/3/howto/unicode.html

Unicode and You
　　betterexplained.com/articles/unicode/

Unicode on Wikipedia
　　en.wikipedia.org/wiki/Unicode

Unicode Normalization on Wikipedia
    en.wikipedia.org/wiki/Unicode_equivalence#Normalization

"A Guide to Unicode"
    youtube.com/watch?v=olhKTHFYNxA

str.casefold Documentation
    docs.python.org/3/library/stdtypes.html#str.casefold

unicodedata Module
    docs.python.org/3/library/unicodedata.html

Free-Range

loc.py

```python
import pandas as pd

df = pd.DataFrame([
    [1, 1, 1],
    [2, 2, 2],
    [3, 3, 3],
    [4, 4, 4],
    [5, 5, 5],
])

print(len(df.loc[1:3]))
```

Guess the Output

Try to guess what the output is before moving to the next page.

This code will print: 3

Slices in Python are half-open ranges. You get values from the first index, up to but not including the last index:

```
In [1]: chars = ['a', 'b', 'c', 'd', 'e']
In [2]: chars[1:3]
Out[2]: ['b', 'c']
```

And most of the time, Pandas words the same way:

```
In [3]: s = pd.Series(chars)
In [4]: s[1:3]
Out[4]:
1    b
2    c
dtype: object
```

There are three ways to slice a pandas.Series or a pandas.DataFrame:

- Using loc, which works by label
- Using iloc, which works by offset
- Using a slice notation (e.g., s[1:3]), which works like iloc

loc works by label and it slices on a closed range, including the last index:

```
In [5]: df[1:3]
Out[5]:
   0  1  2
1  2  2  2
2  3  3  3
In [6]: df.iloc[1:3]
Out[6]:
   0  1  2
1  2  2  2
2  3  3  3
In [7]: df.loc[1:3]
Out[7]:
   0  1  2
1  2  2  2
2  3  3  3
3  4  4  4
```

Watch out for this off-by-one error when using .loc.

Further Reading

loc in Pandas Documentation
    pandas.pydata.org/pandas-docs/stable/reference/api/pandas.DataFrame.loc.html

iloc in Pandas Documentation
pandas.pydata.org/pandas-docs/stable/reference/api/pandas.DataFrame.iloc.html

Indexing and Selecting Data in the Pandas Documentation
pandas.pydata.org/pandas-docs/stable/user_guide/indexing.html

Off-by-One Error on Wikipedia
en.wikipedia.org/wiki/Off-by-one_error

Y3K

future.py

```python
import pandas as pd

y3k = pd.Timestamp(3000, 1, 1)
print(f'They arrived to Earth on {y3k:%B %d}.')
```

Guess the Output

Try to guess what the output is before moving to the next page.

This code will raise an OutOfBoundsDatetime exception.

Computers and time have a complicated relationship. There are daylight saving time, leap years, time zones, and more details to work out.

Computers store time as the number of seconds since January 1, 1970, GMT.

2038

 This means that in 2038, time will overflow on 32-bit machines. Ouch!

Python's datetime and pandas.Timestamp, which is based on it, are written mostly in C and have a fixed amount of space for storing time information. This means there's a maximal and minimal value to datetime.

```
In [1]: pd.Timestamp.min
Out[1]: Timestamp('1677-09-21 00:12:43.145225')
In [2]: pd.Timestamp.max
Out[2]: Timestamp('2262-04-11 23:47:16.854775807')
```

The date we're giving in this teaser is more than the maximal pandas.Timestamp value. This is documented in the "Timestamp Limitations" section in the Pandas documentation.

Further Reading

pandas.Timestamp Documentation
> pandas.pydata.org/pandas-docs/stable/reference/api/pandas.Timestamp.html

"Timeseries Limitations" in the Pandas Documentation
> pandas.pydata.org/pandas-docs/stable/user_guide/timeseries.html#timestamp-limitations

Falsehoods Programmers Believe About Time
> infiniteundo.com/post/25326999628/falsehoods-programmers-believe-about-time

Unix Time on Wikipedia
> en.wikipedia.org/wiki/Unix_time

Year 2038 Problem on Wikipedia
> en.wikipedia.org/wiki/Year_2038_problem

Working with Time Series in the "Python Data Science Handbook" by Jake VanderPlas
> jakevdp.github.io/PythonDataScienceHandbook/03.11-working-with-time-series.html

Not My Type

concat.py

```
import pandas as pd

df1 = pd.DataFrame([[1, 2], [3, 4]], columns=['a', 'b'])
df2 = pd.DataFrame([[5, 6], [7, 8]], columns=['b', 'c'])
df = pd.concat([df1, df2])
print(df.dtypes)
```

Guess the Output

 Try to guess what the output is before moving to the next page.

This code will print:

```
a    float64
b      int64
c    float64
dtype: object</code></pre></td>
```

If you look at the dtypes of df1 and df2, you'll see they are int64:

```
In [1]: df1.dtypes
Out[1]:
a    int64
b    int64
dtype: object
In [2]: df2.dtypes
Out[2]:
b    int64
c    int64
dtype: object
```

Why did the teaser output show the a and c columns as float64?

pandas.concat can handle frames with different columns. By default it will assume there are nan values in the missing labels for a specific column. As we saw in the puzzle *A Delicious Div Sum*, Pandas will change the dtype of a series to allow missing values. And that's what's happening here.

Further Reading

pandas.concat in the Pandas Documentation
> pandas.pydata.org/pandas-docs/stable/reference/api/pandas.concat.html

Merge, Join, and Concatenate in the Pandas Documentation
> pandas.pydata.org/pandas-docs/stable/user_guide/merging.html

Working with Missing Data in the Pandas Documentation
> pandas.pydata.org/pandas-docs/stable/user_guide/missing_data.html

Off with Their NaNs

```python
import numpy as np
import pandas as pd

s = pd.Series([1, np.nan, 3])
print(s[~(s == np.nan)])
```

Guess the Output

 Try to guess what the output is before moving to the next page.

This code will print:

```
0    1.0
1    NaN
2    3.0
dtype: float64
```

We covered some of the floating-point oddities in the puzzle *Multiplying*. NaN (or np.nan) is another oddity. The name NaN stands for *not a number*. It serves two purposes: illegal computation and missing values.

Here's an example of a bad computation:

```
In [1]: np.float64(0)/np.float64(0)
  RuntimeWarning: invalid value encountered in \
  double_scalars np.float64(0)/np.float64(0)
Out[1]: nan
```

You see a warning but not an exception, and the return value is nan.

nan does not equal any number, *including itself*.

```
In [2]: np.nan == np.nan
Out[2]: False
```

To check that a value is nan, you need to use a special function such as pandas.isnull:

```
In [3]: pd.isnull(np.nan)
Out[3]: True
```

You can use pandas.isnull to fix this teaser.

not_nan_fixed.py
```
import numpy as np
import pandas as pd

s = pd.Series([1, np.nan, 3])
print(s[~pd.isnull(s)])
```

pandas.isnull works with all Pandas "missing" values: None, pandas.NaT (not a time), and the new pandas.NA.

Floating points have several other special "numbers" such as inf (infinity), -inf, -0, +0, and others. You can learn more about them in the following links.

Further Reading

pandas.isnull in the Pandas Documentation
    pandas.pydata.org/pandas-docs/stable/reference/api/pandas.isnull.html

Experimental NA Scalar to Denote Missing Values in the Pandas Documentation
pandas.pydata.org/pandas-docs/stable/user_guide/missing_data.html#missing-data-na

Floating-Point Arithmetic: Issues and Limitations in the Python Documentation
docs.python.org/3/tutorial/floatingpoint.html

floating point zine by Julia Evans
twitter.com/b0rk/status/986424989648936960

What Every Computer Scientist Should Know About Floating-Point Arithmetic
docs.oracle.com/cd/E19957-01/806-3568/ncg_goldberg.html

Holding out for a Hero

heros.py

```
import pandas as pd

heros = pd.Series(['Batman', 'Wonder Woman', 'Superman'])
if heros.str.find('Iron Man').any():
    print('Wrong universe')
else:
    print('DC')
```

Guess the Output

 Try to guess what the output is before moving to the next page.

This code will print: Wrong universe

The str.find documentation says the following:

> Return the lowest index in the string where substring *sub* is found within the slice s[start:end]. Optional arguments *start* and *end* are interpreted as in slice notation. Return -1 if *sub* is not found.

In the *Rectified* puzzle, we saw that, except for zeros, all numbers' Boolean values are True.

When you run

```
In [1]: heros.str.find('Iron Man')
Out[1]:
0   -1
1   -1
2   -1
dtype: int64
```

the pandas.Series.any method will return True if at least one of the values in the series is True. Since we have -1 as values, any will return True.

One way to solve this is to use the == operator:

```
In [2]: (heros == 'Iron Man').any()
Out[2]: False
```

Further Reading

str.find in the Python Documentation
    docs.python.org/3/library/stdtypes.html#str.find

pandas.Series.any in the Pandas Documentation
    pandas.pydata.org/pandas-docs/stable/reference/api/pandas.Series.any.html

Truth Value Testing in the Python Documentation
    docs.python.org/3/library/stdtypes.html#truth-value-testing

It's a Date!

```
import pandas as pd

start = pd.Timestamp.fromtimestamp(0).strftime('%Y-%m-%d')
times = pd.date_range(start=start, freq='M', periods=2)
print(times)
```

Guess the Output

Try to guess what the output is before moving to the next page.

This code will print:

```
DatetimeIndex(['1970-01-31', '1970-02-28'], dtype='datetime64[ns]', freq='M')
```

There are two things that are puzzling here:

- M is a month frequency.
- First date is January 31 and not January 1.

Let's start with M being a month frequency. You've probably used the infamous strftime or its cousin strptime to convert datetime to or from strings. There, M stands for minute:

```
In [1]: t = pd.Timestamp(2020, 5, 10, 14, 21, 30)
In [2]: t.strftime('%H:%M')
Out[2]: '14:21'
```

One of the things I like about Pandas is that it's one of the best-documented open source packages out there. But Pandas is a *big* library, and sometimes it's hard to find what you're looking for.

If you look at the pandas.date_range documentation, you'll see the following:

> *freqstr or DateOffset, default 'D'*
> Frequency strings can have multiples, e.g., '5H'. See *here* for a list of frequency aliases.

When you click "here" on the web page, you'll see the full list of what's called DateOffset and you'll see that M stands for *month end frequency*. Minute frequency is T or min.

This solves one puzzle and also gives us a hint about why we see January 31 and not January 1. Remember that in the puzzle *Y3K*, we saw that time 0, or *epoch time*, is January 1, 1970.

```
In [3]: pd.Timestamp(0)
Out[3]: Timestamp('1970-01-01 00:00:00')
```

If you follow the code of pandas.date_range, you'll see it converts the freq from str to a pandas.DateOffset. Then date_range will use pandas.DataOffset.apply on start. From there it'll add the offset for period times.

Let's emulate this:

```
In [4]: from pandas.tseries.frequencies import to_offset
In [5]: start = pd.Timestamp(0)
In [6]: offset = to_offset('M')
In [7]: offset
```

```
Out[7]: <MonthEnd>
In [8]: t0 = offset.apply(start)
In [9]: t0
Out[9]: Timestamp('1970-01-31 00:00:00')
In [10]: t0 + offset
Out[10]: Timestamp('1970-02-28 00:00:00')
```

This is what we see in this teaser's output.

Note that frequencies don't have to be whole units. The following will give you a date range in five-minute intervals.

```
In [11]: pd.date_range(start=pd.Timestamp(0), periods=3, freq='5T')
Out[21]:
DatetimeIndex(['1970-01-01 00:00:00', '1970-01-01 00:05:00',
               '1970-01-01 00:10:00'],
              dtype='datetime64[ns]', freq='5T')
```

Further Reading

strftime() and strptime() Behavior in the Python Documentation
    docs.python.org/3/library/datetime.html#strftime-strptime-behavior

Offset Aliases in the Pandas Documentation
    pandas.pydata.org/pandas-docs/stable/user_guide/timeseries.html#timeseries-offset-aliases

DateOffset in the Pandas Documentation
    pandas.pydata.org/pandas-docs/stable/reference/api/pandas.tseries.offsets.DateOffset.html

Time Series / Date Functionality in the Pandas Documentation
    pandas.pydata.org/pandas-docs/stable/user_guide/timeseries.html

What's the Points?

points.py

```
import pandas as pd

df = pd.DataFrame([[1, 2], [3, 4]], columns=['x', 'y'])
print(df.to_csv())
```

Guess the Output

Try to guess what the output is before moving to the next page.

This code will print:

```
,x,y
0,1,2
1,3,4</code></pre></td>
```

What's with the unnamed column that has 0 and 1 values?

The pandas.DataFrame documentation says:

> Data structure also contains labeled axes (rows and columns). Arithmetic operations align on both row and column labels. Can be thought of as a dict-like container for Series objects. The primary pandas data structure.

The labeled axis for rows is called the *index*.

When you convert a pandas.DataFrame to another format (e.g., CSV, SQL, ...), it will add the index by default.

Use index=False to omit the index.

```
In [1]: print(df.to_csv(index=False))
x,y
1,2
3,4
```

Further Reading

pandas.DataFrame.to_csv in the Pandas Documentation
    pandas.pydata.org/pandas-docs/stable/reference/api/pandas.DataFrame.to_csv.html

IO Tools in the Pandas User Guide
    pandas.pydata.org/pandas-docs/stable/user_guide/io.html

Comma-Separated Values on Wikipedia
    en.wikipedia.org/wiki/Comma-separated_values

Find Me a Phone Booth

identities.py

```python
import pandas as pd

df1 = pd.DataFrame({
    'id': [1, 2, 3],
    'name': ['Clark Kent', 'Diana Prince', 'Bruce Wayne'],
})

df2 = pd.DataFrame({
    'id': [2, 1, 4],
    'hero': ['Wonder Woman', 'Superman', 'Aquaman'],
})

df = pd.merge(df1, df2, on='id')
print(df)
```

Guess the Output

Try to guess what the output is before moving to the next page.

This code will print:

```
    id          name           hero
0   1    Clark Kent        Superman
1   2   Diana Prince   Wonder Woman</code></pre></td>
```

Pandas merge[1] gets a sequence of pandas.DataFrame to merge and an optional column to merge on. If the column is not provided, Pandas will use the index of each DataFrame for merging.

The question is, what happens when one merge column has values that the other doesn't? This question is an old one and is rooted in relational databases and their join[2] operator. There are several types of joins. Each type defines a different behavior. The Pandas merge function mimics these operators as well.

Looking at pandas.merge documentation, you'll see a how parameter:

how {'left', 'right', 'outer', 'inner'}, default 'inner'

Type of merge to be performed.

- left: Use only keys from left frame, similar to a SQL left outer join; preserve key order.

- right: Use only keys from right frame, similar to a SQL right outer join; preserve key order.

- outer: Use union of keys from both frames, similar to a SQL full outer join; sort keys lexicographically.

- inner: Use intersection of keys from both frames, similar to a SQL inner join; preserve the order of the left keys.

The default merge type is inner, which means only rows that have keys in both left and right are included in the result.

merge orders the rows by the order of keys on the left frame. The teaser's output shows the above behavior.

In the output, you see only Superman and Wonder Woman, which have keys in both frames. The output is sorted according to the order of the first frame.

If you switch the order of frames passed to merge, you'll see a different ordering:

---

1.   https://pandas.pydata.org/pandas-docs/stable/reference/api/pandas.merge.html#pandas.merge
2.   https://en.wikipedia.org/wiki/Join_(SQL)

```
In [1]: pd.merge(df2, df1)
Out[1]:
   id          hero          name
0   2  Wonder Woman  Diana Prince
1   1      Superman    Clark Kent
```

If you want to include all lines, use an outer merge. Pandas will fill missing values with NaN:

```
In [2]: pd.merge(df1, df2, on='id', how='outer')
Out[2]:
   id          name          hero
0   1    Clark Kent      Superman
1   2  Diana Prince  Wonder Woman
2   3   Bruce Wayne           NaN
3   4           NaN       Aquaman
```

Pandas merge is very powerful and will let you connect different frames.

A common case from data marts is a *star schema* where you have one main frame with data (called a *fact*) and many other frames that provide auxiliary data.

For example, the main frame will have sale events with customer ID. If you want to group by customer age, you need first to merge the main frame with a customers frame that has customer age for every customer ID. In this case, you'll use a left join.

Further Reading

Merge, Join, and Concatenate in the Pandas Documentation
    pandas.pydata.org/pandas-docs/stable/user_guide/merging.html

Join (SQL) on Wikipedia
    en.wikipedia.org/wiki/Join_(SQL)

Data Mart on Wikipedia
    en.wikipedia.org/wiki/Data_mart

Star Schema on Wikipedia
    en.wikipedia.org/wiki/Star_schema

Chain of Commands

```python
import pandas as pd

df = pd.DataFrame([
    ['133.43.96.45', pd.Timedelta('3s')],
    ['133.68.18.180', pd.Timedelta('2s')],
    ['133.43.96.45', pd.NaT],
    ['133.43.96.45', pd.Timedelta('4s')],
    ['133.43.96.45', pd.Timedelta('2s')],
], columns=['ip', 'duration'])

by_ip = (
    df['duration']
    .fillna(pd.Timedelta(seconds=1))
    .groupby(df['ip'])
    .sum()
)
print(by_ip)
```

Guess the Output

Try to guess what the output is before moving to the next page.

This code will print:

```
ip
133.43.96.45    00:00:10
133.68.18.180   00:00:02
Name: duration, dtype: timedelta64[ns]</code></pre></td>
```

The surprising fact here is that it's valid Python code.

Python's use of white space is pretty unique in programming languages. Some people don't like it. I find it makes the code more readable.

The Python documentation says

> A logical line is constructed from one or more physical lines by following the explicit or implicit line joining rules.

And a bit later

> Expressions in parentheses, square brackets, or curly braces can be split over more than one physical line without using backslashes.

Which means

- 'a' 'b' is not valid.
- ('a', 'b') is a tuple (a, b is also a tuple).
- ('a' 'b') is the string 'ab'.

You can use this *implicit line joining* to make your code clearer and do *method chaining* for complex operations. That is what we do in this teaser.

pandas.DataFrame has a pipe method for use in chaining.

When constructing lists or tuples in multiple lines, you should add a dangling comma (also called *trailing comma* or *final comma*).

```
colors = [
    'red',
    'green'
    'blue',  # ← A dangling comma
]
```

Not only will it save you from bugs, there will be only one line change in code reviews if you add another color. Sadly, not every language or format allows dangling commas. I'm looking at you JSON and SQL.

Further Reading

Lexical Analysis in the Python Documentation
    docs.python.org/3/reference/lexical_analysis.html

Method Chaining in Tom Augspurger's "Modern Pandas"
    tomaugspurger.github.io/method-chaining

Line Structure in the Python Reference
    docs.python.org/3/reference/lexical_analysis.html#line-structure

When to Use Trailing Commas in Python's Style Guide (aka PEP 8)
    python.org/dev/peps/pep-0008/#when-to-use-trailing-commas

Tuple Syntax on the Python Wiki
    wiki.python.org/moin/TupleSyntax

"That Trailing Comma" by Dave Cheney
    dave.cheney.net/2014/10/04/that-trailing-comma

Late Addition

archer.py

```
import pandas as pd

df = pd.DataFrame([
    ['Sterling', 83.4],
    ['Cheryl', 97.2],
    ['Lana', 13.2],
], columns=['name', 'sum'])
df.late_fee = 3.5
print(df)
```

Guess the Output

Try to guess what the output is before moving to the next page.

This code will print:

```
    name       sum
0   Sterling 83.4
1   Cheryl    97.2
2   Lana      13.2
```

Where did the late_fee column go?

Python's objects are very dynamic. You can add attributes to most of them as you please.

```
In [1]: class Point:
   ...:        def __init__(self, x, y):
   ...:            self.x, self.y = x, y
In [2]: p = Point(1, 2)
In [3]: p.x, p.y
Out[3]: (1, 2)
In [4]: p.z = 3
In [5]: p.z
Out[5]: 3
```

Pandas lets you access columns both by square brackets (e.g., df[name]) and by attribute (e.g., df.name). I recommend using square brackets at all times. One reason is, as we saw, when you add an attribute to a DataFrame, it does not register as a new column. Another reason is that column names in CSV, JSON, and other formats can contain spaces or other characters that are not valid Python identifiers, meaning you won't be able to access them with attribute access. df.product id will fail while df['product id'] will work.

And the last reason is that it's confusing:

```
In [6]: df.sum
Out[6]:
<bound method DataFrame.sum of          name    sum
0   Sterling   83.4
1     Cheryl   97.2
2       Lana   13.2>
```

You get the DataFrame sum method and not the sum column. Also:

```
In [7]: df.late_fee
Out[7]: 3.5
```

You probably expected late_fee to be a Series like the other columns.

Sometimes you'd like to add metadata to a DataFrame, say, the name of the file the data was read from.

Instead of adding a new attribute, for example, df.originating_file = '/path/to/sales.db', there's an experimental attribute called attrs for storing metadata in a DataFrame.

```
In [8]: df.attrs['originating_file'] = '/path/to/sales.db'
In [9]: df.attrs
Out[9]: {'originating_file': '/path/to/sales.db'}
```

Further Reading

Indexing Basics in the Pandas Documentation
> pandas.pydata.org/docs/user_guide/indexing.html#basics

Identifiers and Keywords in the Python Documentation
> docs.python.org/3/reference/lexical_analysis.html#identifiers

DataFrame.attrs in the Pandas Documentation
> pandas.pydata.org/docs/reference/api/pandas.DataFrame.attrs.html#pandas.DataFrame.attrs

Hit and Run

```
hits.py
import sqlite3
import pandas as pd

conn = sqlite3.connect(':memory:')
conn.executescript('''
CREATE TABLE visits (day DATE, hits INTEGER);
INSERT INTO visits VALUES
    ('2020-07-01', 300),
    ('2020-07-02', 500),
    ('2020-07-03', 900);
''')

df = pd.read_sql('SELECT * FROM visits', conn)
print('time span:', df['day'].max() - df['day'].min())
```

Guess the Output

 Try to guess what the output is before moving to the next page.

This code will raise a TypeError.

I *love* SQLite3. It's a great single-file database that I've used many times to transfer data. It is widely used and heavily tested and can handle vast amounts of data (currently about 140 terabytes).

However, you need to know how to work with it.

In the teaser code, we create a hits table that has two columns:

- day with SQL DATE type
- hits with SQL INTEGER type

The mapping from SQL types to Python (and Pandas) types is defined in the SQL driver used to access the database. SQLite is a bit different from other databases. Natively, SQLite has only numbers and strings as types, but it does support declaring a column as having a DATE, TIME, or TIMESTAMP type.

You can see that if you look at the .dtypes:

```
In [1]: df.dtypes
Out[1]:
day      object
hits      int64
dtype: object
```

The day column has an object dtype, which in most cases means it's a str. When you do df['day'].max() - df['day'].min(), you're subtracting two strings, which is not a legal operation in Python.

You can convert a column to a Pandas Timestamp either by using the Pandas to_datetime function or by passing the column names to convert in the parse_dates parameter of read_sql. However, you somehow need to know what columns are time.

The better option (IMO) is to use the detect_types parameter in sqlite3.connect. When you pass PARSE_DECLTYPES to sqlite3.connect, it'll convert DATE, TIME, and TIMESTAMP columns to Python's datetime types. read_sql will convert these pandas.Timestamp columns.

Here's the solution:

```
hits_detect.py
import sqlite3
import pandas as pd

conn = sqlite3.connect(
        ':memory:',
        detect_types=sqlite3.PARSE_DECLTYPES,
)
conn.executescript('''
CREATE TABLE visits (day DATE, hits INTEGER);
INSERT INTO visits VALUES
    ('2020-07-01', 300),
    ('2020-07-02', 500),
    ('2020-07-03', 900);
''')

df = pd.read_sql('SELECT * FROM visits', conn)
print('time span:', df['day'].max() - df['day'].min())
```

Further Reading

SQL Queries in the Pandas Documentation
> pandas.pydata.org/pandas-docs/stable/user_guide/io.html#sql-queries

SQLite and Python Types in the Python Documentation
> docs.python.org/3.8/library/sqlite3.html#sqlite-and-python-types

How SQLite Is Tested
> sqlite.org/testing.html

pandas.to_datetime in the Pandas Documentation
> pandas.pydata.org/pandas-docs/stable/reference/api/pandas.to_datetime.html

sqlite3.connect in the Python Documentation
> docs.python.org/3.8/library/sqlite3.html#sqlite3.connect

Index

Thank you!

How did you enjoy this book? Please let us know. Take a moment and email us at support@pragprog.com with your feedback. Tell us your story and you could win free ebooks. Please use the subject line "Book Feedback."

Ready for your next great Pragmatic Bookshelf book? Come on over to https://pragprog.com and use the coupon code BUYANOTHER2021 to save 30% on your next ebook.

Void where prohibited, restricted, or otherwise unwelcome. Do not use ebooks near water. If rash persists, see a doctor. Doesn't apply to *The Pragmatic Programmer* ebook because it's older than the Pragmatic Bookshelf itself. Side effects may include increased knowledge and skill, increased marketability, and deep satisfaction. Increase dosage regularly.

And thank you for your continued support,

The Pragmatic Bookshelf

Python Brain Teasers

We geeks love puzzles and solving them. The Python programming language is a simple one, but like all other languages it has quirks. This book uses those quirks as teaching opportunities via 30 simple Python programs that challenge your understanding of Python. The teasers will help you avoid mistakes, see gaps in your knowledge, and become better at what you do. Use these teasers to impress your co-workers or just to pass the time in those boring meetings. Teasers are fun!

Miki Tebeka
(80 pages) ISBN: 9781680509007. $9
https://pragprog.com/book/d-pybrain

Go Brain Teasers

This book contains 25 short programs that will challenge your understanding of Go. Like any big project, the Go developers had to make some design decisions that at times seem surprising. This book uses those quirks as a teaching opportunity. By understanding the gaps in your knowledge, you'll become better at what you do. Some of the teasers are from the author's experience shipping bugs to production, and some from others doing the same. Teasers and puzzles are fun, and learning how to solve them can teach you to avoid programming mistakes and maybe even impress your colleagues and future employers.

Miki Tebeka
(78 pages) ISBN: 9781680508994. $18.95
https://pragprog.com/book/d-gobrain

Complex Network Analysis in Python

Construct, analyze, and visualize networks with networkx, a Python language module. Network analysis is a powerful tool you can apply to a multitude of datasets and situations. Discover how to work with all kinds of networks, including social, product, temporal, spatial, and semantic networks. Convert almost any real-world data into a complex network—such as recommendations on co-using cosmetic products, muddy hedge fund connections, and online friendships. Analyze and visualize the network, and make business decisions based on your analysis. If you're a curious Python programmer, a data scientist, or a CNA specialist interested in mechanizing mundane tasks, you'll increase your productivity exponentially.

Dmitry Zinoviev
(260 pages) ISBN: 9781680502695. $35.95
https://pragprog.com/book/dzcnapy

Intuitive Python

Developers power their projects with Python because it emphasizes readability, ease of use, and access to a meticulously maintained set of packages and tools. The language itself continues to improve with every release: writing in Python is full of possibility. But to maintain a successful Python project, you need to know more than just the language. You need tooling and instincts to help you make the most out of what's available to you. Use this book as your guide to help you hone your skills and sculpt a Python project that can stand the test of time.

David Muller
(140 pages) ISBN: 9781680508239. $26.95
https://pragprog.com/book/dmpython

Genetic Algorithms and Machine Learning for Programmers

Self-driving cars, natural language recognition, and online recommendation engines are all possible thanks to Machine Learning. Now you can create your own genetic algorithms, nature-inspired swarms, Monte Carlo simulations, cellular automata, and clusters. Learn how to test your ML code and dive into even more advanced topics. If you are a beginner-to-intermediate programmer keen to understand machine learning, this book is for you.

Frances Buontempo
(234 pages) ISBN: 9781680506204. $45.95
https://pragprog.com/book/fbmach

Programming Machine Learning

You've decided to tackle machine learning — because you're job hunting, embarking on a new project, or just think self-driving cars are cool. But where to start? It's easy to be intimidated, even as a software developer. The good news is that it doesn't have to be that hard. Master machine learning by writing code one line at a time, from simple learning programs all the way to a true deep learning system. Tackle the hard topics by breaking them down so they're easier to understand, and build your confidence by getting your hands dirty.

Paolo Perrotta
(340 pages) ISBN: 9781680506600. $47.95
https://pragprog.com/book/pplearn

Hands-on Rust

Rust is an exciting new programming language combining the power of C with memory safety, fearless concurrency, and productivity boosters—and what better way to learn than by making games. Each chapter in this book presents hands-on, practical projects ranging from "Hello, World" to building a full dungeon crawler game. With this book, you'll learn game development skills applicable to other engines, including Unity and Unreal.

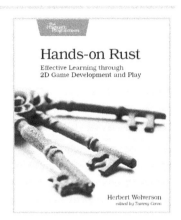

Herbert Wolverson

(342 pages) ISBN: 9781680508161. $47.95

https://pragprog.com/book/hwrust

Python Testing with pytest, Second Edition

Test applications, packages, and libraries large and small with pytest, Python's most powerful testing framework. pytest helps you write tests quickly and keep them readable and maintainable. In this fully revised edition, explore pytest's superpowers—simple asserts, fixtures, parametrization, markers, and plugins—while creating simple tests and test suites against a small database application. Using a robust yet simple fixture model, it's just as easy to write small tests with pytest as it is to scale up to complex functional testing. This book shows you how.

Brian Okken

(250 pages) ISBN: 9781680508604. $

https://pragprog.com/book/bopytest2

Kotlin and Android Development featuring Jetpack

Start building native Android apps the modern way in Kotlin with Jetpack's expansive set of tools, libraries, and best practices. Learn how to create efficient, resilient views with Fragments and share data between the views with ViewModels. Use Room to persist valuable data quickly, and avoid NullPointerExceptions and Java's verbose expressions with Kotlin. You can even handle asynchronous web service calls elegantly with Kotlin coroutines. Achieve all of this and much more while building two full-featured apps, following detailed, step-by-step instructions.

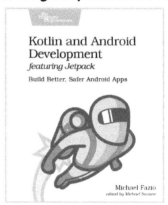

Michael Fazio
(444 pages) ISBN: 9781680508154. $49.95
https://pragprog.com/book/mfjetpack

Learn to Program, Third Edition

It's easier to learn how to program a computer than it has ever been before. Now everyone can learn to write programs for themselves—no previous experience is necessary. Chris Pine takes a thorough, but lighthearted approach that teaches you the fundamentals of computer programming, with a minimum of fuss or bother. Whether you are interested in a new hobby or a new career, this book is your doorway into the world of programming.

Chris Pine
(230 pages) ISBN: 9781680508178. $45.95
https://pragprog.com/book/ltp3

Practical Programming, Third Edition

Classroom-tested by tens of thousands of students, this new edition of the best-selling intro to programming book is for anyone who wants to understand computer science. Learn about design, algorithms, testing, and debugging. Discover the fundamentals of programming with Python 3.6—a language that's used in millions of devices. Write programs to solve real-world problems, and come away with everything you need to produce quality code. This edition has been updated to use the new language features in Python 3.6.

Paul Gries, Jennifer Campbell, Jason Montojo
(410 pages) ISBN: 9781680502688. $49.95
https://pragprog.com/book/gwpy3

Modern CSS with Tailwind

Tailwind CSS is an exciting new CSS framework that allows you to design your site by composing simple utility classes to create complex effects. With Tailwind, you can style your text, move your items on the page, design complex page layouts, and adapt your design for devices from a phone to a wide-screen monitor. With this book, you'll learn how to use the Tailwind for its flexibility and its consistency, from the smallest detail of your typography to the entire design of your site.

Noel Rappin
(90 pages) ISBN: 9781680508185. $26.95
https://pragprog.com/book/tailwind

The Pragmatic Bookshelf

The Pragmatic Bookshelf features books written by professional developers for professional developers. The titles continue the well-known Pragmatic Programmer style and continue to garner awards and rave reviews. As development gets more and more difficult, the Pragmatic Programmers will be there with more titles and products to help you stay on top of your game.

Visit Us Online

This Book's Home Page
https://pragprog.com/book/d-pandas
Source code from this book, errata, and other resources. Come give us feedback, too!

Keep Up to Date
https://pragprog.com
Join our announcement mailing list (low volume) or follow us on twitter @pragprog for new titles, sales, coupons, hot tips, and more.

New and Noteworthy
https://pragprog.com/news
Check out the latest pragmatic developments, new titles and other offerings.

Save on the ebook

Save on the ebook versions of this title. Owning the paper version of this book entitles you to purchase the electronic versions at a terrific discount.

PDFs are great for carrying around on your laptop—they are hyperlinked, have color, and are fully searchable. Most titles are also available for the iPhone and iPod touch, Amazon Kindle, and other popular e-book readers.

Send a copy of your receipt to support@pragprog.com and we'll provide you with a discount coupon.

Contact Us

Online Orders:	*https://pragprog.com/catalog*
Customer Service:	*support@pragprog.com*
International Rights:	*translations@pragprog.com*
Academic Use:	*academic@pragprog.com*
Write for Us:	*http://write-for-us.pragprog.com*
Or Call:	+1 800-699-7764

Lightning Source UK Ltd.
Milton Keynes UK
UKHW032243051021
391725UK00002B/7